Be You!
Jill D. Clark

For Noah and Eleanor

In memory of
Susan, Bruce, Carol and Troy

©2018 by Jill D. Clark

authorjillclark.com

Illustrated by Lynda Farrington Wilson
lyndafarringtonwilson.com

Printed in China

ISBN: 978-1-7324294-0-6

If I Had Eleven Toes...

BY Jill D. Clark

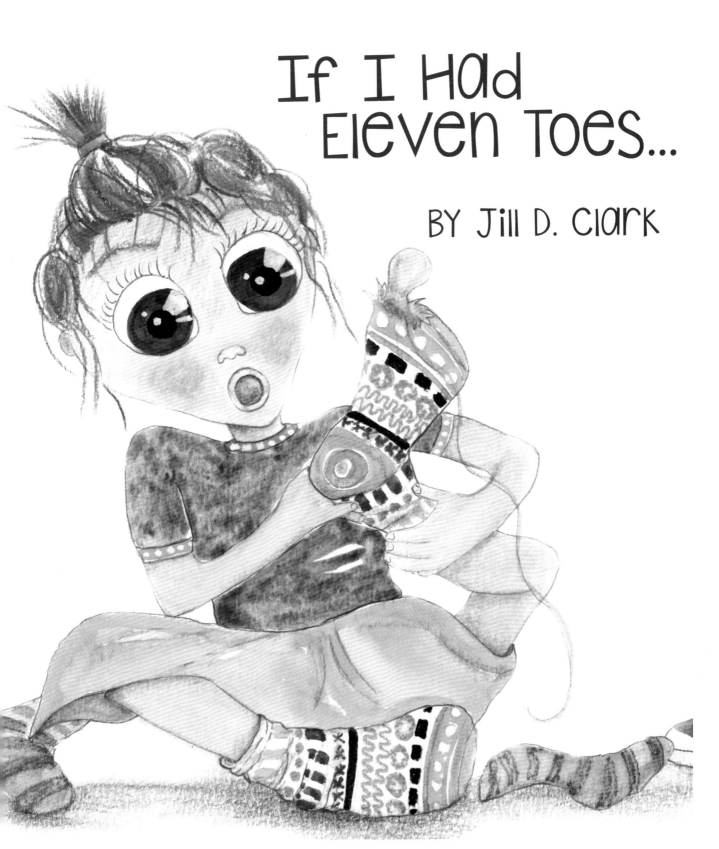

Illustrated by Lynda Farrington Wilson

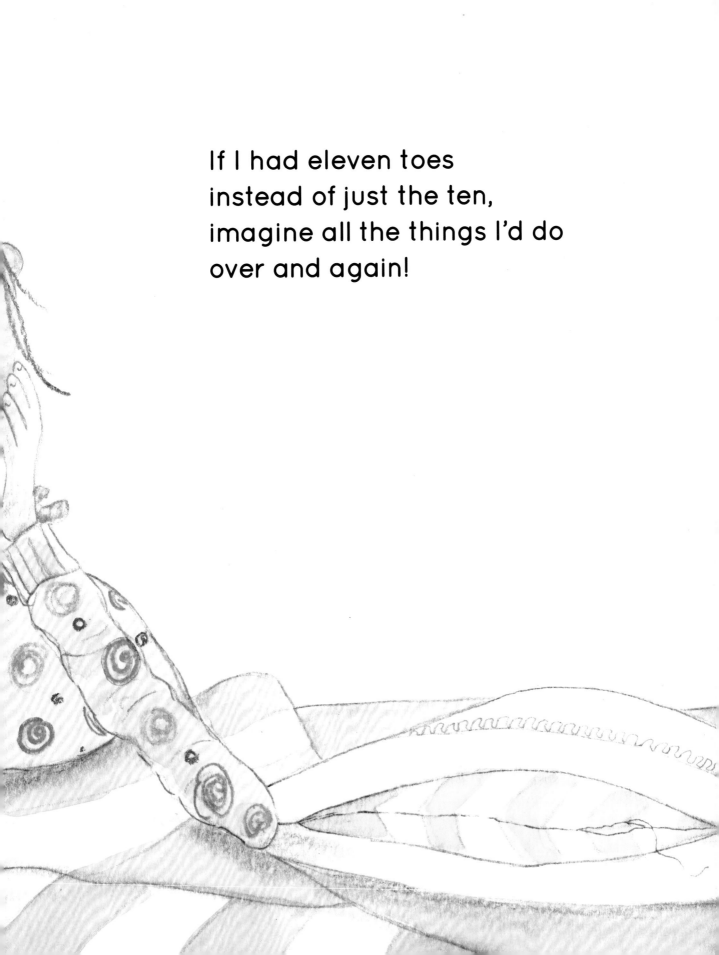

If I had eleven toes
instead of just the ten,
imagine all the things I'd do
over and again!

I'd zoom along at lightning pace.
I'd beat a cheetah in a race.

I'd outrun all the kids at school,
outswim a dolphin in a pool...

...swing like a monkey in a zoo,
jump higher than a kangaroo!

I'd be a giant superstar,
travel the world
both near and far...

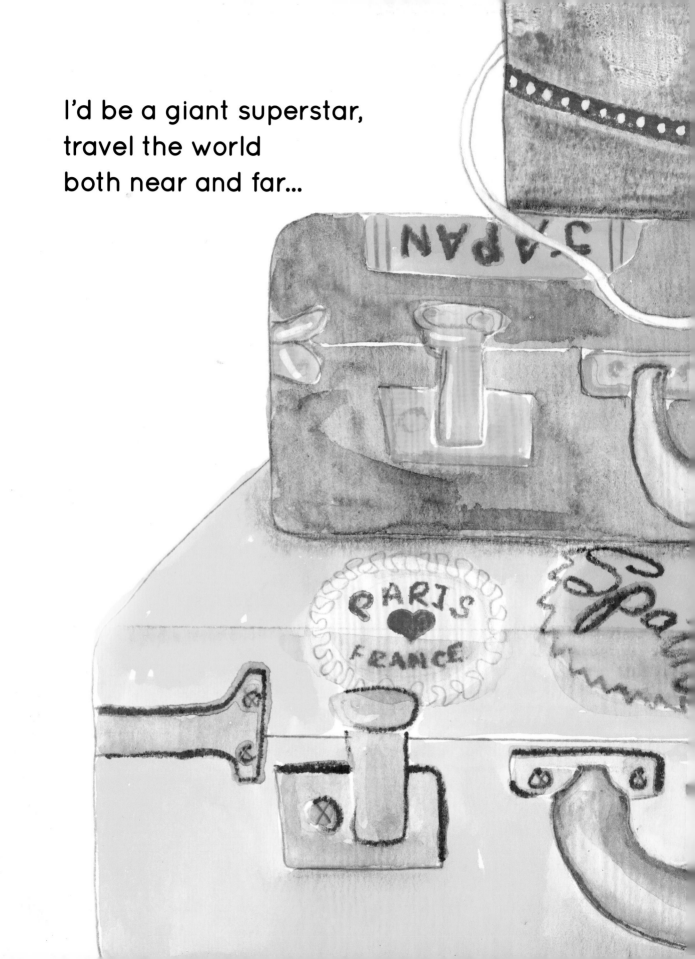

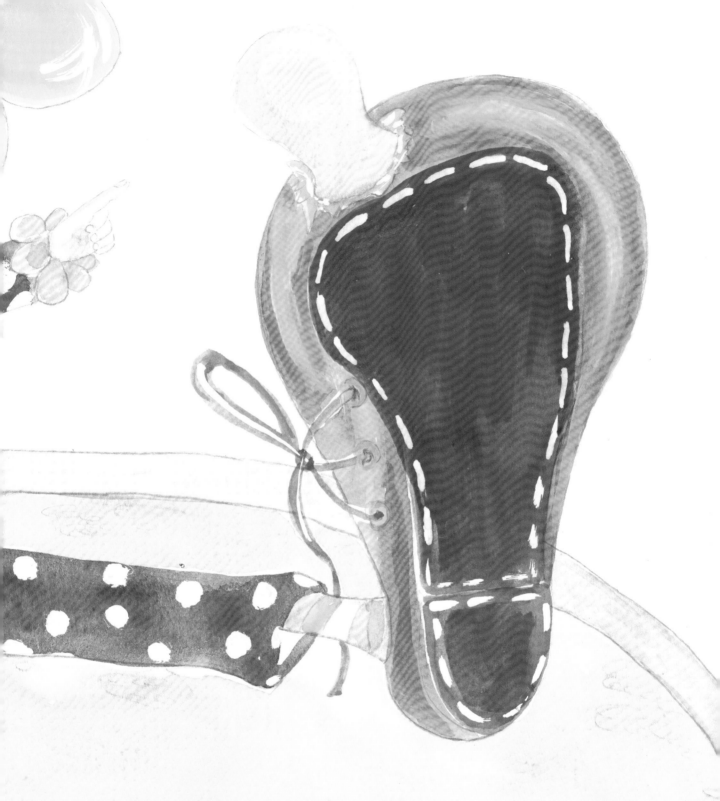

...or join the circus as a clown.
I'd be the biggest talk of town!

It's clear I have
this figured out.
There's not one little
shred of doubt
that everyone
would want to be
eleven toed just like me!

But if I had an extra toe,
would socks and shoes still fit?

Oh no!

Or would I have
two strange left feet
when dancing to
a rhythmic beat?

What would I call
my extra toe?
Pinky, or Moe
or Curly Joe?

Would it be big
or maybe small?
I haven't got
a clue at all!

To market would that piggy go?
Or stay at home and just lay low?

Would that toe eat roast beef or not?
Oh gee my brain is in a knot!

I guess having an extra toe
is not the greatest way to go.
I'm glad I have just ten, you see.

I'm happy I'm exactly ME!

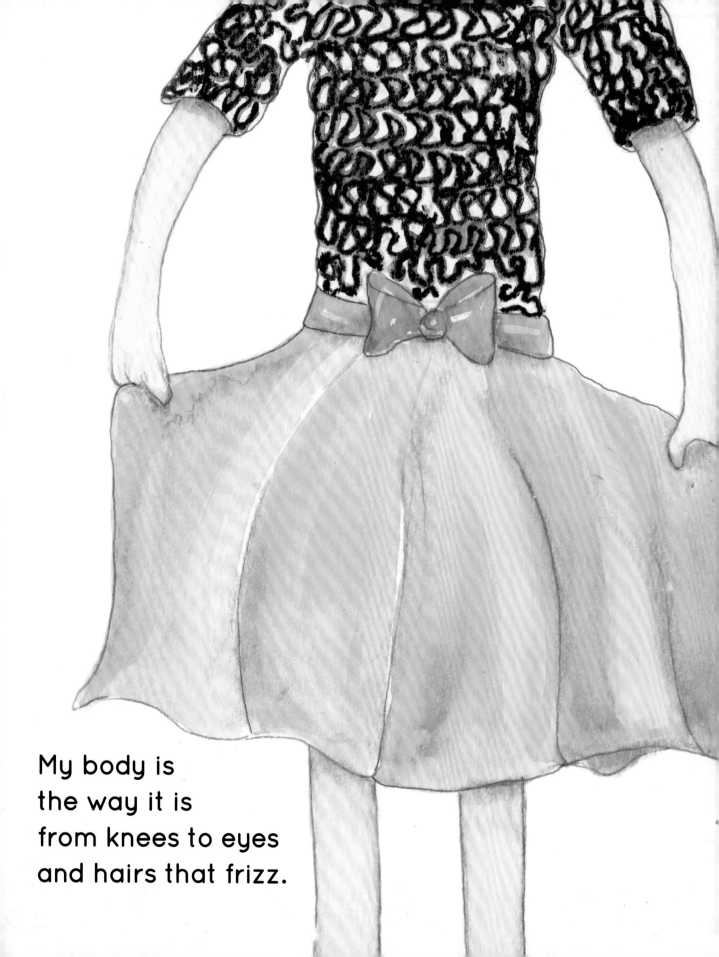

My body is
the way it is
from knees to eyes
and hairs that frizz.

But one
more thing
I've asked
for years.

What if I had...

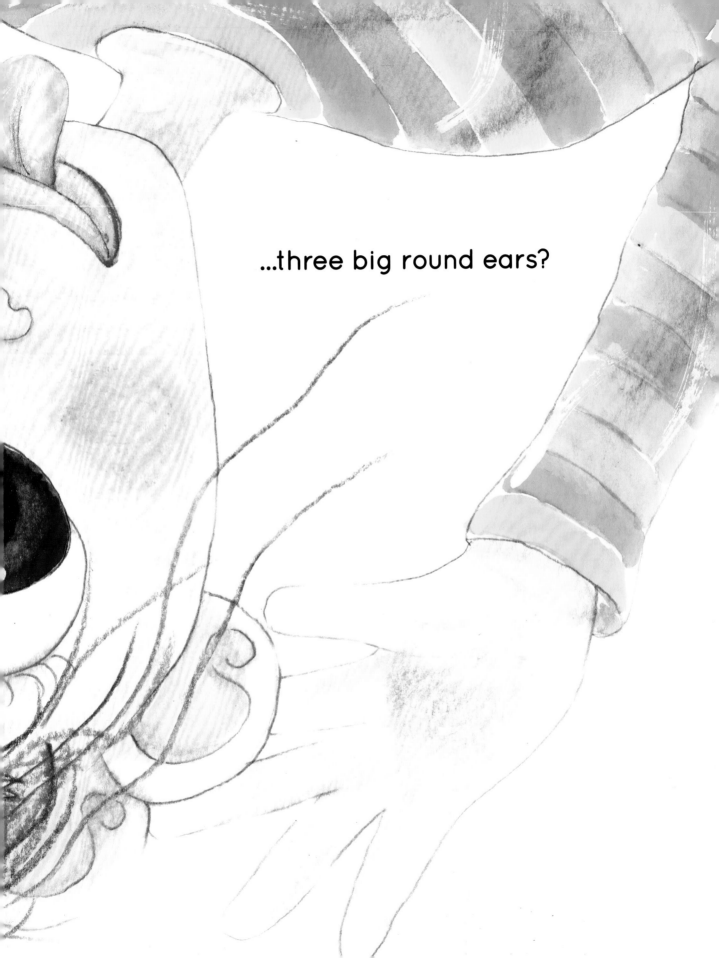

About The Author

Jill Clark is a God-fearing, out-door-loving, Netflix-binging, friend and family-obsessed parent of twins, Noah and Eleanor. She is married to her fabulous husband, Brent, and together they live in St. Louis, Missouri, with said goofball twins.

Jill has been writing professionally for nearly 10 years, specifically in the world of education. Her writing has appeared in chapter books, edited volumes, journals, magazines and blogs.

If I Had Eleven Toes is Jill's first venture into children's writing.